POETRY FROM CRESCENT MOON

William Shakespeare: *The Sonnets*
edited and introduced by Mark Tuley

*Shakespeare: Love, Poetry and Magic
in Shakespeare's Sonnets and Plays*
by B.D. Barnacle

Edmund Spenser: *Heavenly Love: Selected Poems*
selected and introduced by Teresa Page

Robert Herrick: *Delight In Disorder: Selected Poems*
edited and introduced by M.K. Pace

Sir Thomas Wyatt: *Love For Love: Selected Poems*
selected and introduced by Louise Cooper

John Donne: *Air and Angels: Selected Poems*
selected and introduced by A.H. Ninham

D.H. Lawrence: *Being Alive: Selected Poems*
edited with an introduction by Margaret Elvy

D.H. Lawrence: Symbolic Landscapes
by Jane Foster

D.H. Lawrence: Infinite Sensual Violence
by M.K. Pace

Percy Bysshe Shelley: *Paradise of Golden Lights: Selected Poems*
selected and introduced by Charlotte Greene

Thomas Hardy: *Her Haunting Ground: Selected Poems*
edited, with an introduction by A.H. Ninham

Sexing Hardy: Thomas Hardy and Feminism
by Margaret Elvy

Emily Bronte: *Darkness and Glory: Selected Poems*
selected and introduced by Miriam Chalk

John Keats: *Bright Star: Selected Poems*
edited with an introduction by Miriam Chalk

Henry Vaughan: *A Great Ring of Pure and Endless Light:
Selected Poems*
selected and introduced by A.H. Ninham

You Burn Me
Poems

You Burn Me

Poems

Sappho

Translated by J.M. Edmonds
Edited by Louise Cooper

CRESCENT MOON

CRESCENT MOON PUBLISHING
P.O. Box 1312, Maidstone
Kent, ME14 5XU
Great Britain, www.crmooncom

First published 2008. Revised 2014, 2016.
Introduction © Louise Cooper 2008, 2014, 2016.

Printed and bound in the U.S.A.
Set in Garamond Book 12 on 16pt.
Designed by Radiance Graphics.

ISBN-13 9781861711519
ISBN-13 9781861715418

Contents

Acknowledgements

To William Heinemann for *Lyra Graeca*, edited by J.M. Edmonds (second, enlarged edition, 1928).

Charles Mengin, Sappho, 1867, Manchester

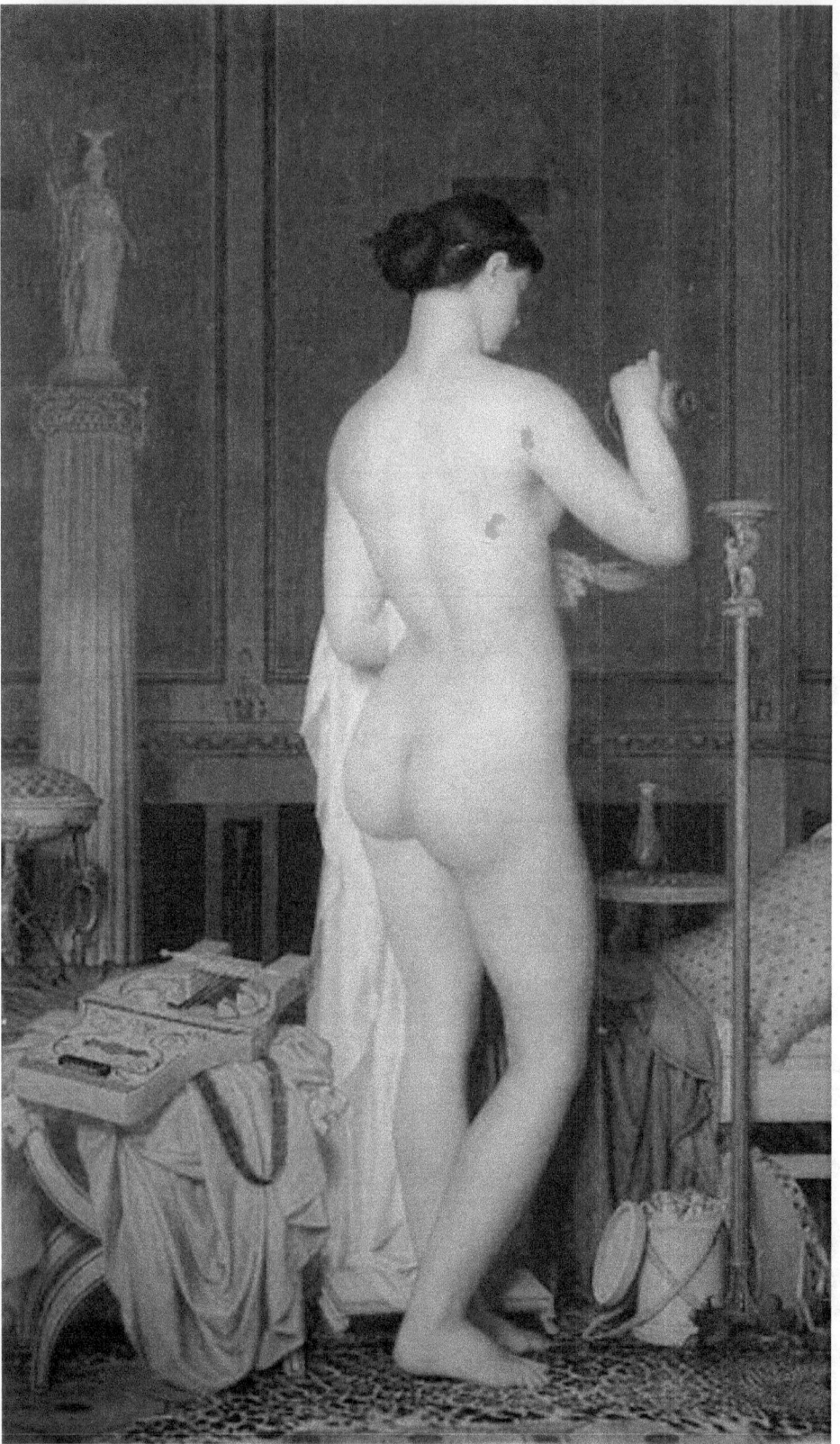

Marc-Charles-Gabriel Gleyre, Le Coucher de Sappho, 1867, Lausanne

1

To Aphrodite

Aphrodite splendour-throned immortal, wile-weaving child of Zeus, to thee is my prayer. Whelm not my heart, O Queen, with suffering and sorrow, but come hither I pray thee, if ever ere this thou hast heard and marked my voice afar, and stepping from thy Father's house harnessed a golden chariot, and the strong pinions of thy two swans fair and swift, whirring from heaven through mid-sky, have drawn thee towards the dark earth, and lo! were there; and thou, blest Lady, with a smile on that immortal face, didst gently ask what ailed me, and why I called, and what this wild heart would have done, and 'Whom shall I make to give thee room in her heart's love, who is it, Sappho, that does thee wrong? for even if she flees thee, she shall soon pursue; if she will not take thy gifts, she yet shall give; and if she loves not, soon love she shall, whether or no;' –
O come to me now as thou camest then, to assuage my sore trouble and do what my heart would fain have done, thyself my stay in battle.

2

It is to be a god, methinks, to sit before you and listen
close by to the sweet accents and winning laughter
which have made the heart in my breast beat fast, I
warrant you. When I look on you, Brocheo, my speech
comes short or fails me quite, I am tongue-tied; in a
moment a delicate fire has overrun my flesh, my eyes
grow dim and my ears sing, the sweat runs down me
and a trembling takes me altogether, till I am as green
and pale as the grass, and death itself seems not very far
away; but now that I am poor, I must fain be content...

3

Around the fair moon the bright beauty of the stars is lost them when her silver light illuminates the world at its fullest.

4

...And by the cool waterside the breeze rustles amid the apple-branches, and the quivering leaves shed lethargy.

6

To Aphrodite

…Come, Queen of Love, to bear round golden cups of nectar mingled with gentle cheer unto these comrades of thine and mine.

12

These songs I will sing right well today for the delight of my comrades.

14

Towards you pretty ones this mind of mine can never change.

23

... and I long and I yearn ...

24

To Hecate

Aphrodite's golden-shining handmaid…

27

...you burn me...

28

giver of pain

weaver of tales

32

To Hesperus

Fairest of all the stars that shine

34

… heart … altogether … [if] I can … shall be to me … shine back … fair face …… engrained …

35

[To Charaxus]

...will give. If you hover about the notable rather than the good and noble and bid your friends go their ways, and grieve me by saying in your swelling pride that I, forsooth, am become a reproach to you, at such things as these you may rejoice your heart. Feed your fill. For as for me, my mind is not so softly disposed to the anger of a child. But make no mistake in this; [the snare never catches the old bird;] I know what was the depth of your knavery before, and of what sort is the foe I am opposed to. Be you better advised then, and change your heart; for well I know that being of a gentle disposition I have the Gods on my side.

36

To the Nereïds

Golden Nereïds, grant me I pray my brother's safe return, and that the true desires of his heart shall be accomplished, and putting away his former errors he shall become a delight to his friends and a grief to his enemies; and may our house be disgraced of no man. And may he be willing to ring honour to his sister; and the sore pain and the words wherewith, in bitter resentment of a taunt that must have cut to the quick, he sought ere he departed to overwhelm my heart, – O, when return he does on some near day, may he choose amid his fellow-townsmen's mirth to cast them clean away, and to have a mate, if he desire one, in wedlock due and worthy; and as for thee, thou black and baleful she-dog, thou mayst set that evil snout to the ground and go a-hunting other prey.

43

And then I answered: 'Gentle dames, how you will evermore remember till you be old, our life together in the heyday of youth! For many things did we then together both pure and beautiful. And now that you depart hence, love wrings my heart with very anguish.'

44

...For when I look upon you, then meseems Hermione was never such as you are, and just it is to liken you rather to Helen than to a mortal maid; nay, I tell you, I render your beauty the sacrifice of all my thoughts and worship you with all my feelings.

45

To Gongyla

[Come hither tonight] I pray, my rosebud Gongyla,
and with your Lydian lyre; surely a desire of my heart
ever hovers about your lovely self; for the sight of your
very robe thrills me, and I rejoice that it is so. Once on a
day, I too found fault with the Cyprus-born...

48

To Atthis

I loved you, Atthis, long ago, when my own girlhood was still all flowers, and you – you seemed to me a small ungainly child.

52

I know not what to do; I am in two minds…

53

I could not expect to touch the sky with my two arms.

54

As for me, love has shaken my wits as a down-rushing whirlwind that falls upon the oaks.

56

...And I will set [you] reclining on soft cushions.

81

To Atthis

Love, the looser of limbs stirs me, that creature irresistible, bitter-sweet; but you, Atthis, have come to hate the thought of me, and run after Andromeda in my stead.

83

[To Atthis?]

[So I shall never see Atthis more,] and in sooth I might
as well be dead. And yet she wept full sore to leave me
behind and said 'Alas! how sad our lot; Sappho, I swear
'tis all against my will I leave thee'; and I answered her,
'Go your way rejoicing and remember me, for you
know how I doted upon you. And if you remember not,
O then I will remind you of what you forget, how dear
and beautiful was the life we led together. For with
many a garland of violets and sweet roses mingled you
have decked your flowing locks by my side, and with
many a woven necklet made of a hundred blossoms
your dainty throat; and with unguent in plenty, both of
the precious and the royal, have you anointed your fair
young skin in my bosom, and upon a soft couch had
from the hands of gentle serving-maids all that a
[delicate-living Ionian] could desire; and no [hill] was
there, nor holy place nor [water-brook], whither we did
not go, nor ever did the [crowded] noise of the [early]
Spring [fill] any wood with the medley-song [of
nightingales, but you wandered thither with me...]

86

[To Atthis]

[Atthis, our beloved Anactoria dwells in far-off] Sardis, but she often sends her thoughts hither, thinking how once we used to live in the days when you were like a glorious Goddess to her and she loved your song the best. And now she shines among the dames of Lydia as after sunset the rosy-fingered Moon beside the stars that are about her, when she spreads her light o'er briny sea and eke o'er flowery field, while the dew lies so fair on the ground and the roses revive and the dainty anthrysc and the melilot with all its blooms. And oftentime while our beloved wanders abroad, when she calls to mind the love of gentle Atthis, her tender breast, for sure, is weighed down deep with longing; and she cries aloud for us to come thither; and what she says we know full well, you and I, for flower-tressed Night that hath the many ears calls it to us along all that lies between.

86A

[To Herself]

Be still, my soul; not for me canst thou send forth with
swift thoughts hymn-outwelling an Adonis-Song whose
beauty shall please the Goddesses. For alas! thou art
made dumb by man-dishonouring Desire and Whelm-
the-Heart Aphrodite; and wit-destroying Persuasion's
ewer of gold hath poured its suave nectar upon thy
understanding.

94

And pours down a sweet shrill song from beneath his wings, when the Sun-god illumines the earth with his down-shed flame outspread.

105

And wrapped her all about with soft cambric.

106

I will have neither honey nor bees

111

The Moon is gone
And the Pleiades set,
  Midnight is nigh;
Time passes on,
And passes; yet
  Alone I lie.

118

...But I love delicacy, and the bright and the beautiful belong for me to the desire of the sunlight.

135

Sweet mother, I truly cannot weave my web; for I am overwhelmed through Aphrodite with love of a slender youth.

149

Evening Star that bringest back all that lightsome
Dawn hath scattered afar, thou bringest the sheep, thou
bringest the goat, thou bringest her child home to the
mother...

158

Thy form, O bride, is all delight; thy eyes are of a
gentle hue; thy fair face is overspread with love;
Aphrodite hath done thee exceeding honour.

Illustrations

Portrayals of Sappho in art.

Sappho Reading, c. 435 B.C., Attic Vase,

Sappho, Greek vase, c. 470 B.C.

Gustave Moreau, Sappho, private collection

Angelica Kauffmann, Sappho, 1774

Théodore Chassériau, Sappho Leaping Into the Sea From the
Leucadian Promontory, c. 1840, Louvre, Paris

Lawrence Alma-Tadema, Sappho and Alcaeus, 1881

John Godward, In the Days of Sappho,
1904, Getty Center, Los Angeles

Jules Elie Delaunay, Sappho Embracing Her Lyre

Charles Lafond, Sappho and Homer, 1824

Giovanni Dupré, Sappho, 1857, Rome

Pierre-Narcisse Guérin, Sappho On the Leucadian Cliff, 1800

Simeon Solomon, Sappho and Erinna
In a Garden At Mytilene, 1864

Gustav Klimt, Sappho, 1888-90

Lawrence Koe (1869-1913), Sappho

Paul Avril, Sappho and Her Girlfriends

A NOTE ON SAPPHO

Sappho has become one of the touchstones of Western poetry, an icon and heroine for poets of any gender. For the simple reason that her poetry is very, very good. Well, not just good, it's genius, the real thing. Sappho has been cited by many many poets, including Lord Byron, Sir Philip Sidney, John Donne, Alexander Pope, John Addison, Dante Gabriel Rossetti, Samuel Taylor Coleridge, Alfred Tennyson, Christina Rossetti, Algernon Swinburne, Thomas Hardy, William Carlos Williams, Allen Tate, Robert Lowell, Lawrence Durrell, Robert Graves, Amy Lowell, Ezra Pound, Edna St Vincent Millay, and many contemporary poets. Sappho has become an icon for lesbian, gay and queer poets and writers. She has been the subject of much critical debate; in the 19th and early 20th centuries, questions of authorship were prominent; in the Eighties and Nineties, Sappho's poetry was absorbed into lesbian and queer theory and poetics.

Aside from the poem to Aphrodite, the rest of Sappho's work is in fragments, sometimes nothing more than a word or a phrase. Sometimes not even the words are complete. Yet her poetic voice shines through the fragments: very sensuous, ironic, self-deprecating, passionate, very lyrical. Her vocabulary is direct and simple, and sometimes colloquial. Edgar Lobel, one of Sappho's celebrated translators, said that her language was 'non-literary'. Her metaphors are powerful, sometimes lush – such as the ecstasy of love being compared to the wind in the oak trees on a mountainside.

The imagery in her poetry is of the natural world, in all its beauty and simplicity, its violence and cruelty. There are images of trees, mountains, streams, the sun and moon, stars, orchards, flowers, breezes, grass, nights, dawns, and the Pleiades. In her poetry one finds evocations of paradisal worlds, with streams, springs, apple trees, sunshine, roses, incense and gardens. Sappho's is a synæsthetic poetry, one which sets alive all the senses, as most of the best poetry does.

Apart from the wealth of nature imagery, the other main area of allusion and reference is to religion – to gods and goddesses, to devotion and prayer, to temples and rituals. The deities and personages of the Classical world permeate Sappho's love poetry: Aphrodite above all, but also Zeus, Helen, Hecate, Hesperus and the Nereïds.

In amongst the fragments and single phrases of Sappho's poetry, one poem stands out, the hymn to Aphrodite. It is largely on this one poem that Sappho's high literary reputation rests. 'The Hymn to Aphrodite' is a very great poem, a poem of worship, awe and desire, with brilliant imagery and metaphors. It's supremely a poem about love, but is also self-mocking and self-conscious.

In Sappho's poetry, love is potentially ecstatic and wild, even though the poet knows that love often ends in bitterness and sadness. Sappho describes the effects of love on her body, the way it brings chills, sweating, weakness, sickness, blurred vision. It is a love poetry firmly grounded in earthy reality, in the physical body and its senses. Sappho's poetry embodies nearly all love poetry, and a very personal kind of love poetry, which revolves around the poetic self, not anyone else. Her poetry records how the emotions and conflicts of love affect herself.

Sappho remains detached and analytical at the same time as she depicts herself acting foolishly in love. She realizes that the description in poems of her loves and hates has a ridiculous and pitiful aspect.

Sappho celebrates love in terms which have become standard, ways which are found throughout Western poetry, from the troubadours and Italian *stil novisti*, to Shakespeare and the Elizabethans, to the Romantics and Symbolists. Sappho creates the now-familiar lover in poetry: who desires despite knowing it will end in bitterness, who yearns for one particular person, whose irony and suspicion cannot prevent her from falling in love, whose intelligence does not stop her from acting foolishly, who is tongue-tied in front of the beloved yet extremely articulate in private. The self-consciousness and emotions of the Sappho lover persona have not dated at all, over two and a half thousand years: Sappho's poetry remains contemporary and modern.

Sappho invented the term 'bitter-sweet' to describe love. She wrote wedding songs. She wrote the first (known) portrayal of a romantic moonlit night (C. Paglia, 1993).

Camille Paglia wrote:

In plain, concise language, Sappho analyzes her extreme state as if she were both actor and observer; she is candid and emotional yet dignified, austere, almost clinical. (C. Paglia, 1993)

Sappho and Alcaeus lived in the island of Lesbos, off the Aeolian coast. Sappho was married with a daughter, but her poetry depicts a poetic persona passionately in love with women. Scholars have disagreed about Sappho's sexuality since ancient times (C. Paglia, 1993).

In some respects, it's not significant at all that Sappho was a woman, a female poet. In other respects, it's very important. Ancient poetry isn't now simply a matter of Dead White Males. There's Homer, and Ovid, and Catullus, and Petronius, and Virgil, and Sophocles (and others) among the celebrated writers of the ancient world, but there is also Sappho. And she is every bit as 'great' as the male writers are.

Plenty of poets through the ages have translated Sappho's poetry, or written poetry inspired by her work or her example, or composed variations on her poems. Among those who've rendered Sappho into English are Sir Philip Sidney, Ambrose Philips, John Addison, Thomas Hardy, Lord Byron, Dante Gabriel Rossetti, William Carlos Williams, Richard Aldington, and Robert Lowell. Thomas Hardy's 'Sapphic Fragment', for instance, runs thus:

> Dead shalt thou lie; and nought
> Be told of thee or thought,
> For thou hast plucked not of the Muse's tree:
> And even in Hades' halls
> Amidst thy fellow-thralls
> No friendship shade thy shade company!

What's amazing is that Sappho's poetry, like Homer's epic stories, remains as fresh and inspiring today, after two and a half thousand years.

SELECT BIBLIOGRAPHY

SAPPHO

The Poems of Sappho, tr. P. Maurice Hill, Staples Press, 1953
Poetarum Lesbiorum Fragmenta, ed. E. Lobel & D. Page, Oxford, 1955
Sappho and Alcaeus, ed. D. Page, Oxford, 1955
Greek Lyric, tr. D. Campbell, vol. 1, Loeb Classical Library, 1982
Sappho Through English Poetry, ed. Peter Jay & Caroline Lewis, Anvil
   Press Poetry, 1996

OTHERS

Willis Barnstone, ed. *Greek Lyric Poetry*, Schocken Books, New York,
   1972
—. & Aliki Barnstone, eds. *A Book of Women Poets: From Antiquity to
   Now*, Schocken Books, New York, 1980
C.M. Bowra. *Greek Lyric Poetry*, Oxford, 1961
J.M. Edmonds, ed. *Lyra Graeca*, Heinemann, 1928
John F. Nims. *Sappho to Valery: Poems in Translation,* Princeton
   University Press, 1980
Camille Paglia, "Love Poetry", in A. Preminger & T. Bogan, eds. *The
   Princeton Encyclopedia of Poetry and Poetics*, Princeton University
   Press, 1993.
M.L. West. *Greek Lyric Poetry*, Oxford University Press, 1993
M. Williamson. *Sappho's Immortal Daughters*, London, 1995

Life, Life
Selected Poems

Arseny Tarkovsky

translated and edited by Virginia Rounding

Arseny Tarkovsky is the neglected Russian poet, father of the acclaimed film director Andrei Tarkovsky. This new book gathers together many of Tarkovsky's most lyrical and heartfelt poems, in Rounding's clear, new translations. Many of Tarkovsky's poems appeared in his son's films, such as *Mirror, Stalker, Nostalghia* and *The Sacrifice*. There is an introduction by Rounding, and a bibliography of both Arseny and Andrei Tarkovsky.

Bibliography and notes 124pp 3rd ed ISBN 9781861712660 Hbk ISBN 9781861711144

Beauties, Beasts, and Enchantment

CLASSIC FRENCH FAIRY TALES

Translated and with an Introduction
by Jack Zipes

A collection of 36 classic French fairy tales translated by renowned writer Jack Zipes.
Cinderella, Beauty and the Beast, Sleeping Beauty and *Little Red Riding Hood* are among the
classic fairy tales in this amazing book.
Includes illustrations from fairy tale collections.
Jack Zipes has written and published widely on fairy tales.

'Terrific... a succulent array of 17th and 18th century 'salon' fairy tales'
- *The New York Times Book Review*

'These tales are adventurous, thrilling in a way fairy tales are meant to be... The translation
from the French is modern, happily free of archaic and hyperbolic language... a fine and
sophisticated collection' - *New York Tribune*

'Enjoyable to read... a unique collection of French regional folklore' - *Library Journal*

'Charming stories accompanied by attractive pen-and-ink drawings' - *Chattanooga Times*

Introduction and illustrations 612pp.   ISBN 9781861712510 Pbk ISBN 9781861713193 Hbk

MAURICE SENDAK

& the art of children's book illustration

Maurice Sendak is the widely acclaimed American children's book author and illustrator. This critical study focuses on his famous trilogy, *Where the Wild Things Are*, *In the Night Kitchen* and *Outside Over There*, as well as the early works and Sendak's superb depictions of the Grimm Brothers' fairy tales in *The Juniper Tree*. L.M. Poole begins with a chapter on children's book illustration, in particular the treatment of fairy tales. Sendak's work is situated within the history of children's book illustration, and he is compared with many contemporary authors.

Fully illustrated. The book has been revised and updated for this edition.
ISBN 9781861714282 Pbk   ISBN 9781861713469 Hbk

In the Dim Void

Samuel Beckett's Late Trilogy:
Company, Ill Seen, Ill Said and
Worstward Ho

by Gregory Johns

This book discusses the luminous beauty and dense, rigorous poetry of Samuel Beckett's late works, *Company, Ill Seen, Ill Said* and *Worstward Ho*. Gregory Johns looks back over Beckett's long writing career, charting the development from the *Molloy-Malone Dies-Unnamable* trilogy through the 'fizzles' of the 1960s to the elegiac lyricism of the *Company* series. Johns compares the trilogy with late plays such as *Ghosts, Footfalls* and *Rockaby*.

Bibliography, notes. Illustrated. 120pp
ISBN 9781861712974 Pbk and ISBN 9781861712608 Hbk
9781861713407 E-book

CRESCENT MOON PUBLISHING

web: www.crmoon.com e-mail: cresmopub@yahoo.co.uk

ARTS, PAINTING, SCULPTURE

The Art of Andy Goldsworthy
Andy Goldsworthy: Touching Nature
Andy Goldsworthy in Close-Up
Andy Goldsworthy: Pocket Guide
Andy Goldsworthy In America
Land Art: A Complete Guide
The Art of Richard Long
Richard Long: Pocket Guide
Land Art In the UK
Land Art in Close-Up
Land Art In the U.S.A.
Land Art: Pocket Guide
Installation Art in Close-Up
Minimal Art and Artists In the 1960s and After
Colourfield Painting
Land Art DVD, TV documentary
Andy Goldsworthy DVD, TV documentary
The Erotic Object: Sexuality in Sculpture From Prehistory to the Present Day
Sex in Art: Pornography and Pleasure in Painting and Sculpture
Postwar Art
Sacred Gardens: The Garden in Myth, Religion and Art
Glorification: Religious Abstraction in Renaissance and 20th Century Art
Early Netherlandish Painting
Leonardo da Vinci
Piero della Francesca
Giovanni Bellini
Fra Angelico: Art and Religion in the Renaissance
Mark Rothko: The Art of Transcendence
Frank Stella: American Abstract Artist
Jasper Johns
Brice Marden
Alison Wilding: The Embrace of Sculpture
Vincent van Gogh: Visionary Landscapes
Eric Gill: Nuptials of God
Constantin Brancusi: Sculpting the Essence of Things
Max Beckmann
Caravaggio
Gustave Moreau
Egon Schiele: Sex and Death In Purple Stockings
Delizioso Fotografico Fervore: Works In Process I
Sacro Cuore: Works In Process 2
The Light Eternal: J.M.W. Turner
The Madonna Glorified: Karen Arthurs

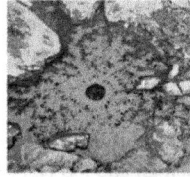

LITERATURE

J.R.R. Tolkien: The Books, The Films, The Whole Cultural Phenomenon
J.R.R. Tolkien: Pocket Guide
Tolkien's Heroic Quest
The *Earthsea* Books of Ursula Le Guin
Beauties, Beasts and Enchantment: Classic French Fairy Tales
German Popular Stories by the Brothers Grimm
Philip Pullman and *His Dark Materials*
Sexing Hardy: Thomas Hardy and Feminism
Thomas Hardy's *Tess of the d'Urbervilles*
Thomas Hardy's *Jude the Obscure*
Thomas Hardy: The Tragic Novels
Love and Tragedy: Thomas Hardy
The Poetry of Landscape in Hardy
Wessex Revisited: Thomas Hardy and John Cowper Powys
Wolfgang Iser: Essays and Interviews
Petrarch, Dante and the Troubadours
Maurice Sendak and the Art of Children's Book Illustration
Andrea Dworkin
Cixous, Irigaray, Kristeva: The *Jouissance* of French Feminism
Julia Kristeva: Art, Love, Melancholy, Philosophy, Semiotics and Psychoanalysis
Hélène Cixous I Love You: The *Jouissance* of Writing
Luce Irigaray: Lips, Kissing, and the Politics of Sexual Difference
Peter Redgrove: Here Comes the Flood
Peter Redgrove: Sex-Magic-Poetry-Cornwall
Lawrence Durrell: Between Love and Death, East and West
Love, Culture & Poetry: Lawrence Durrell
Cavafy: Anatomy of a Soul
German Romantic Poetry: Goethe, Novalis, Heine, Hölderlin
Feminism and Shakespeare
Shakespeare: Love, Poetry & Magic
The Passion of D.H. Lawrence
D.H. Lawrence: Symbolic Landscapes
D.H. Lawrence: Infinite Sensual Violence
Rimbaud: Arthur Rimbaud and the Magic of Poetry
The Ecstasies of John Cowper Powys
Sensualism and Mythology: The Wessex Novels of John Cowper Powys
Amorous Life: John Cowper Powys and the Manifestation of Affectivity (H.W. Fawkner)
Postmodern Powys: New Essays on John Cowper Powys (Joe Boulter)
Rethinking Powys: Critical Essays on John Cowper Powys
Paul Bowles & Bernardo Bertolucci
Rainer Maria Rilke
Joseph Conrad: *Heart of Darkness*
In the Dim Void: Samuel Beckett
Samuel Beckett Goes into the Silence
André Gide: Fiction and Fervour
Jackie Collins and the Blockbuster Novel
Blinded By Her Light: The Love-Poetry of Robert Graves
The Passion of Colours: Travels In Mediterranean Lands
Poetic Forms

POETRY

Ursula Le Guin: Walking In Cornwall
Peter Redgrove: Here Comes The Flood
Peter Redgrove: Sex-Magic-Poetry-Cornwall
Dante: Selections From the Vita Nuova
Petrarch, Dante and the Troubadours
William Shakespeare: Sonnets
William Shakespeare: Complete Poems
Blinded By Her Light: The Love-Poetry of Robert Graves
Emily Dickinson: Selected Poems
Emily Brontë: Poems
Thomas Hardy: Selected Poems
Percy Bysshe Shelley: Poems
John Keats: Selected Poems
Joh n Keats: Poems of 1820
D.H. Lawrence: Selected Poems
Edmund Spenser: Poems
Edmund Spenser: Amoretti
John Donne: Poems
Henry Vaughan: Poems
Sir Thomas Wyatt: Poems
Robert Herrick: Selected Poems
Rilke: Space, Essence and Angels in the Poetry of Rainer Maria Rilke
Rainer Maria Rilke: Selected Poems
Friedrich Hölderlin: Selected Poems
Arseny Tarkovsky: Selected Poems
Arthur Rimbaud: Selected Poems
Arthur Rimbaud: A Season in Hell
Arthur Rimbaud and the Magic of Poetry
Novalis: Hymns To the Night
German Romantic Poetry
Paul Verlaine: Selected Poems
Elizaethan Sonnet Cycles
D.J. Enright: By-Blows
Jeremy Reed: Brigitte's Blue Heart
Jeremy Reed: Claudia Schiffer's Red Shoes
Gorgeous Little Orpheus
Radiance: New Poems
Crescent Moon Book of Nature Poetry
Crescent Moon Book of Love Poetry
Crescent Moon Book of Mystical Poetry
Crescent Moon Book of Elizabethan Love Poetry
Crescent Moon Book of Metaphysical Poetry
Crescent Moon Book of Romantic Poetry
Pagan America: New American Poetry

MEDIA, CINEMA, FEMINISM and CULTURAL STUDIES

J.R.R. Tolkien: The Books, The Films, The Whole Cultural Phenomenon
J.R.R. Tolkien: Pocket Guide
The Lord of the Rings Movies: Pocket Guide
The Cinema of Hayao Miyazaki
Hayao Miyazaki: Princess Mononoke: Pocket Movie Guide
Hayao Miyazaki: Spirited Away: Pocket Movie Guide
Tim Burton : Hallowe'en For Hollywood
Ken Russell
Ken Russell: Tommy: Pocket Movie Guide
The Ghost Dance: The Origins of Religion
The Peyote Cult
Cixous, Irigaray, Kristeva: The Jouissance of French Feminism
Julia Kristeva: Art, Love, Melancholy, Philosophy, Semiotics and Psychoanalysis
Luce Irigaray: Lips, Kissing, and the Politics of Sexual Difference
Hélene Cixous I Love You: The Jouissance of Writing
Andrea Dworkin
'Cosmo Woman': The World of Women's Magazines
Women in Pop Music
HomeGround: The Kate Bush Anthology
Discovering the Goddess (Geoffrey Ashe)
The Poetry of Cinema
The Sacred Cinema of Andrei Tarkovsky
Andrei Tarkovsky: Pocket Guide
Andrei Tarkovsky: Mirror: Pocket Movie Guide
Andrei Tarkovsky: The Sacrifice: Pocket Movie Guide
Walerian Borowczyk: Cinema of Erotic Dreams
Jean-Luc Godard: The Passion of Cinema
Jean-Luc Godard: Hail Mary: Pocket Movie Guide
Jean-Luc Godard: Contempt: Pocket Movie Guide
Jean-Luc Godard: Pierrot le Fou: Pocket Movie Guide
John Hughes and Eighties Cinema
Ferris Bueller's Day Off: Pocket Movie Guide
Jean-Luc Godard: Pocket Guide
The Cinema of Richard Linklater
Liv Tyler: Star In Ascendance
Blade Runner and the Films of Philip K. Dick
Paul Bowles and Bernardo Bertolucci
Media Hell: Radio, TV and the Press
An Open Letter to the BBC
Detonation Britain: Nuclear War in the UK
Feminism and Shakespeare
Wild Zones: Pornography, Art and Feminism
Sex in Art: Pornography and Pleasure in Painting and Sculpture
Sexing Hardy: Thomas Hardy and Feminism

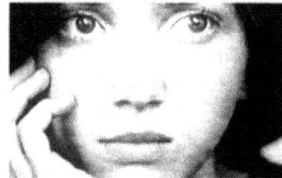

The Light Eternal is a model monograph, an exemplary job. The subject matter of the book is beautifully organised and dead on beam. (Lawrence Durrell)
It is amazing for me to see my work treated with such passion and respect. (Andrea Dworkin)

CRESCENT MOON PUBLISHING
P.O. Box 1312, Maidstone, Kent, ME14 5XU, Great Britain. www.crmoon.com

cresmopub@yahoo.co.uk   www.crescentmoon.org.uk

www.ingramcontent.com/pod-product-compliance
Lightning Source LLC
Chambersburg PA
CBHW072046040426
42447CB00012BB/3048